# Doctor by Day, Ninja by Night

## TEACHING ANTONYMS

BY LISA OWINGS

# The Child's World®
## childsworld.com

Published by The Child's World®
1980 Lookout Drive • Mankato, MN 56003-1705
800-599-READ • www.childsworld.com

ACKNOWLEDGMENTS
The Child's World®: Mary Swensen, Publishing Director
Red Line Editorial: Editorial direction and production
The Design Lab: Design

Photographs ©: Yulia Glam/Shutterstock Images, cover (left),
2-3; Shutterstock Images, cover (right), 1, 4, 5, 9; Dragon Images/
Shutterstock Images, 6, 6-7; Tom Wang/Shutterstock Images,
8; Dmitry Naumov/Shutterstock Images, 10; Monkey Business
Images/Shutterstock Images, 13; Ami Parikh/Shutterstock Images,
14

ISBN 9781503808362
LCCN 2015958425

Printed in the United States of America
Mankato, MN
June, 2016
PA02304

## ABOUT THE AUTHOR
Lisa Owings has a degree in English and
creative writing from the University of
Minnesota. She has written and edited a wide
variety of educational books for young people.
Lisa lives in Andover, Minnesota.

Antonyms are words with opposite meanings. Look for **antonyms** in this book. You will find them in **bold** type.

Daisy wears a **white** lab coat over **black** clothing. She is a doctor each **day**. At **night** she becomes a ninja!

James is **quiet** in class. But at home he is **loud**! He is **silly** with friends. Only teachers think he is **serious**.

Superhero Amara flies **high** then dips **low**. She looks for **bad** guys to help them be **good**.

Andre's dog Cooper **loves** to cuddle. He **hates** being alone. Cooper looks **mean**. But he is really **nice**.

Marta has soccer practice **near** her home. The tournaments are always **far** away.

Eli writes **short** poems and **long** stories. He thinks of a **beginning**. He keeps writing until the **end**!

## Did you find these antonyms?

bad/good          hates/loves
beginning/        high/low
end               long/short
black/white       loud/quiet
day/night         mean/nice
far/near          serious/silly

## To Learn More

### IN THE LIBRARY

Heinrichs, Ann. *Synonyms and Antonyms*. Mankato, MN: The Child's World, 2011.

Horacek, Petr. *Animal Opposites*. Somerville, MA: Candlewick, 2013.

Johnson, Robin A. *The Word Wizard's Book of Synonyms and Antonyms*. New York: Crabtree, 2015.

### ON THE WEB

Visit our Web site for links about antonyms: **childsworld.com/links**

*Note to Parents, Teachers, and Librarians: We routinely verify our Web links to make sure they are safe and active sites. So encourage your readers to check them out!*